Threading Orbs

AN EXHIBITION OF JACQUARD TAPESTRIES
AND WORKS ON PAPER BY

THIERRY W DESPONT

SEPTEMBER 23 - OCTOBER 23, 2010

Marlborough

40 WEST 57TH STREET
NEW YORK, NEW YORK 10019
212-541-4900
MARLBOROUGHGALLERY.COM

66 In tapestry, a thread is a thin yarn used for weaving. In computer science, a thread is the smallest unit of processing. In this show, I weave a thread from drawing to a computer driven loom to create large tapestries of orbs floating in space."

THIERRY W DESPONT

Do not ask what is it?
Let us go and pay our visit.
In the room women come and go,
Talking of Michelangelo.

T.S. ELIOT

THREADING ORBS

A CONVERSATION BETWEEN THIERRY DESPONT AND DALE LANZONE
AT THE ARTIST'S STUDIO ON JULY 8, 2010

DALE LANZONE: *As a contemporary artist and architect what brought the very ancient tapestry medium to your attention?*

THIERRY DESPONT: I always thought that in architecture or in art, that there is a continuum, it is not new medium versus old. I was especially interested in using a medium as old as tapestry, which has been around for centuries. I curiously thought of it because of drawing. I like drawing on paper; I do it all of the time. I was looking at some of the master draftsmen of the 17th century, such as Le Brun, who created beautiful drawings and cartoons for tapestry. The other reason why I got into tapestry has to do with the technology of today, of computer aided digital photo processes. These technologies, combined with the milling processes, open up whole new avenues of artistic expression. It struck me that Jacquard weaving today operates the same way as it did 300 years ago. There are still thread pickers, dyers, etc., but today a color printer can reproduce any color, and I found a mill in Belgium that can work with ten or so basic thread colors and produce any color one wants, mixing basic color threads like a color painter mixes basic colors to reproduce the entire spectrum.

DL: *This sounds like a complex medium.*

TD: Yes! I thought it would be pretty simple and straightforward but the process...the cartoon first, starting with a large drawing or a full-size cartoon or painting. It has to be full-size, it cannot be blown up due to pixilation. All of the tapestries in the show have started from a full-size cartoon which has been photographed and digitized, and, using the Photoshop program, every pixel has been assigned a value. Then the colors are indexed to make a palette, by indexing I mean finding out which color is the closest to the original cartoon on the palette provided by the mill. Each palette can then be toned. All of the colors can be shaded in one direction or another. First, you work on the computer to compare the shading, color by color. As an artist, you must be rigid in what you want. Then from this palette, the mill gives you a range of 250 colors and you can pick and choose every color and run a test. Eight to ten basic colors of thread, not dyed, and the weave is creating the combinations of these basic threads to get any variation of color. Sometimes the machine will make decisions on its own. Often these are happy accidents. In some cases variation occurs in the weave where there are floats or hanging threads, and this can be desirable. I have done watercolors, mixed media, but in any media, with my training in architecture, I like discipline and control. Tapestry is a medium with enormous possibility, from metallic threads, glass beads, etc., and I realize now that the possibilities of expression are endless. These are not in the show, but I am experimenting with painting on a tapestry or using a sewing machine to embroider over a tapestry, as well as other layering techniques.

DL: *So this would be direct application in the studio?*

TD: Absolutely. I am not interested in doing production pieces, but unique editions.

DL: *Why the planet/orb paintings for this medium?*

TD: I am always interested in large-scale work. In the future, I want to do bigger tapestries, though right now, we are at the width limit of the loom. But tapestries are practical for installations. Instead of transporting and disassembling and reassembling the large paintings, you just roll it! I still want to produce these on a monumental scale, even though we are at the largest width, around 8 feet, this loom in Belgium is one of the largest in the world, but I would still love a 24-foot loom.

DL: *Is production and creation as unique and complex as making a painting?*

TD: Absolutely. I am definitely not interested in series. Each work is unique. I have had many rejects in order to get the final result. When you are satisfied with the first steps on the computer and then you ask for a woven palette, I feel it is like in astronomy, the process of exploring in space, a planet through its light spectrum. Somehow with this process, it is the same, you can see the spectrum analysis of your drawing or painting. We get the light, we analyze the light, and based on the spectrum, you get the image. You analyze the "spectrum" or palette, and then instruct the mill to do test samples. We test various parts of the composition, an area of interest, the edge or the center, looking at the color and the weave variations. We can then adjust both colors and weave. For instance we can have the same color woven differently. As in a painting, you have an idea of what the painting will look like, but you do not really know until you are finished. Tapestry is the same process, you discover the unexpected through testing, a dialogue with the machine to get results or changes.

DL: *And you mentioned the use of metallic threads?*

TD: If I could get some sparkle from a cartoon, how could I do it? We can introduce gold or silver and it is wonderful, not in your face, but giving the tapestry more depth and liveliness. Some have metallic threads and some do not. Another avenue of exploration, which the mill is not thrilled about, is doing a totally metallic tapestry. It is very complex but we will get there.

DL: *They seem to be internally illuminated?*

TD: Yes, I think they glow. I cannot explain it. And especially for the planets. I like to think of my orbs as floating in space, and the three-dimensional aspects of tapestry make it a fantastic medium for them.

DL: *The way the tapestries hold the light, they do not release it back the way a painting does, they absorb the light and then glow.*

TD: I am fascinated by our universe filled with billions of galaxies, of stars and planets, by the notion of being drawn into space and floating away. The tapestries display this poetic notion of floating with these orbs, the light bounces off softly. And people are drawn to them. In the studio, every visitor wants to touch them. It is an emotional force, they exert their own kind of gravity.

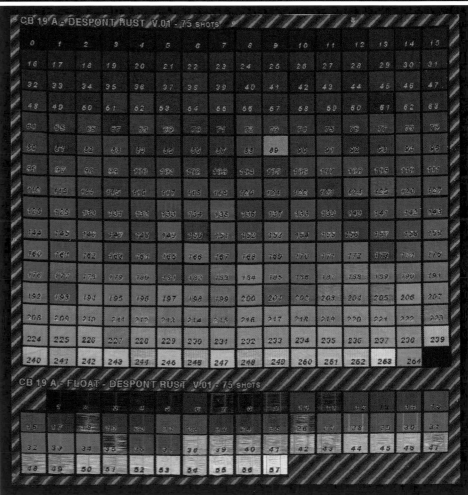

TAPESTRIES

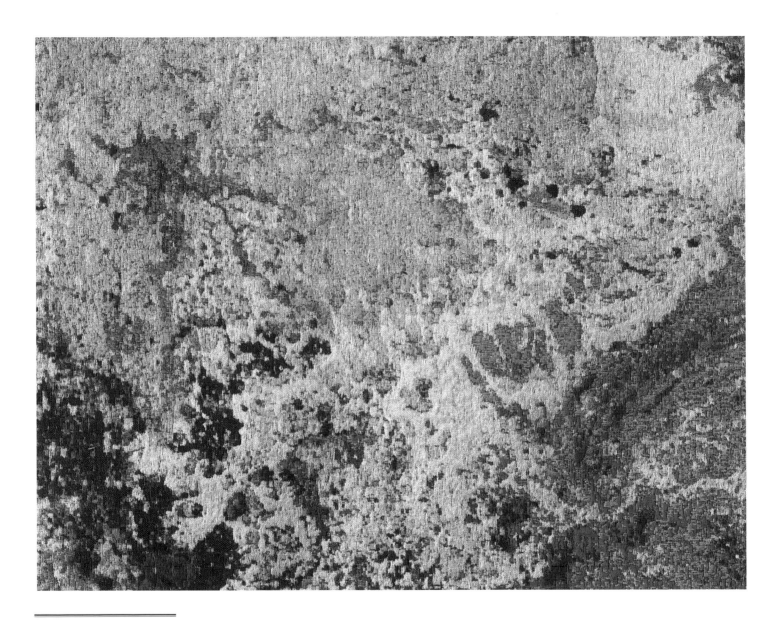

NB 03-T

2010, JACQUARD TAPESTRY

81 X 149 IN., 205.7 X 378.5 CM

OPPOSITE, ABOVE IN DETAIL

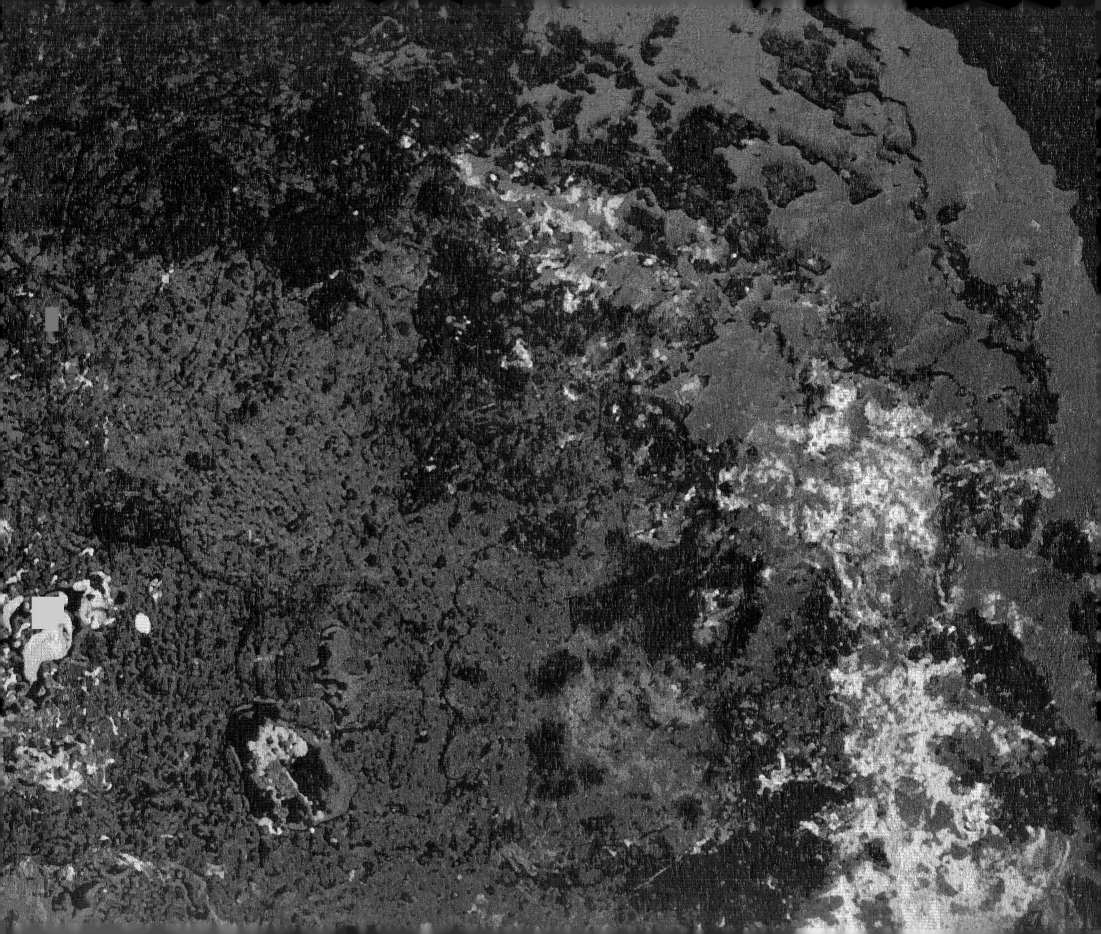

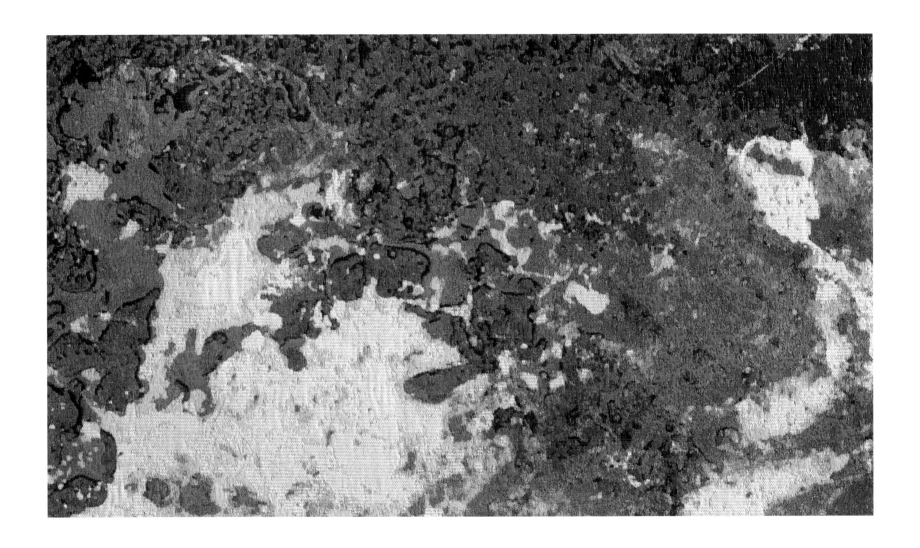

NB 17-T

2010, JACQUARD TAPESTRY
81 X 149 IN., 205.7 X 378.5 CM
REVERSE, ABOVE IN DETAIL

NB 02-T

2010, JACQUARD TAPESTRY

81 X 149 IN., 205.7 X 378.5 CM

OPPOSITE, ABOVE IN DETAIL

NB 09-T

2010, JACQUARD TAPESTRY
81 X 149 IN., 205.7 X 378.5 CM
REVERSE, ABOVE IN DETAIL

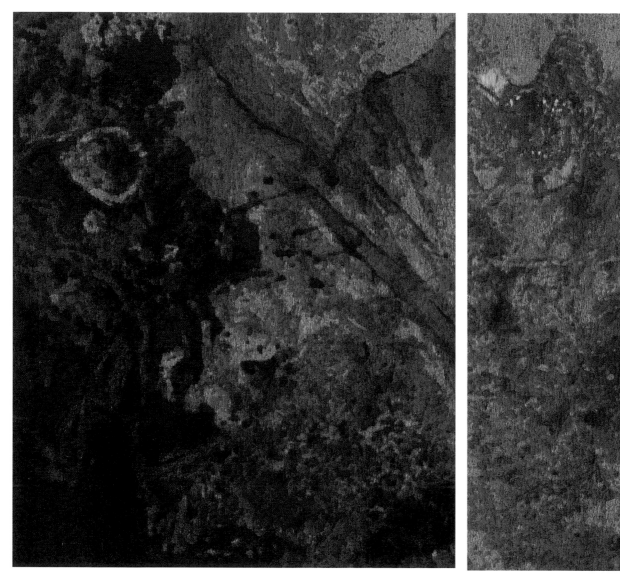
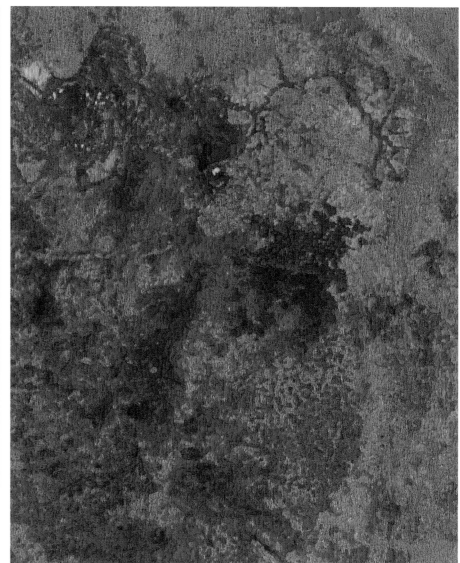

NB 07-T

2010, JACQUARD TAPESTRY

81 X 149 IN., 205.7 X 378.5 CM

OPPOSITE, ABOVE IN DETAIL

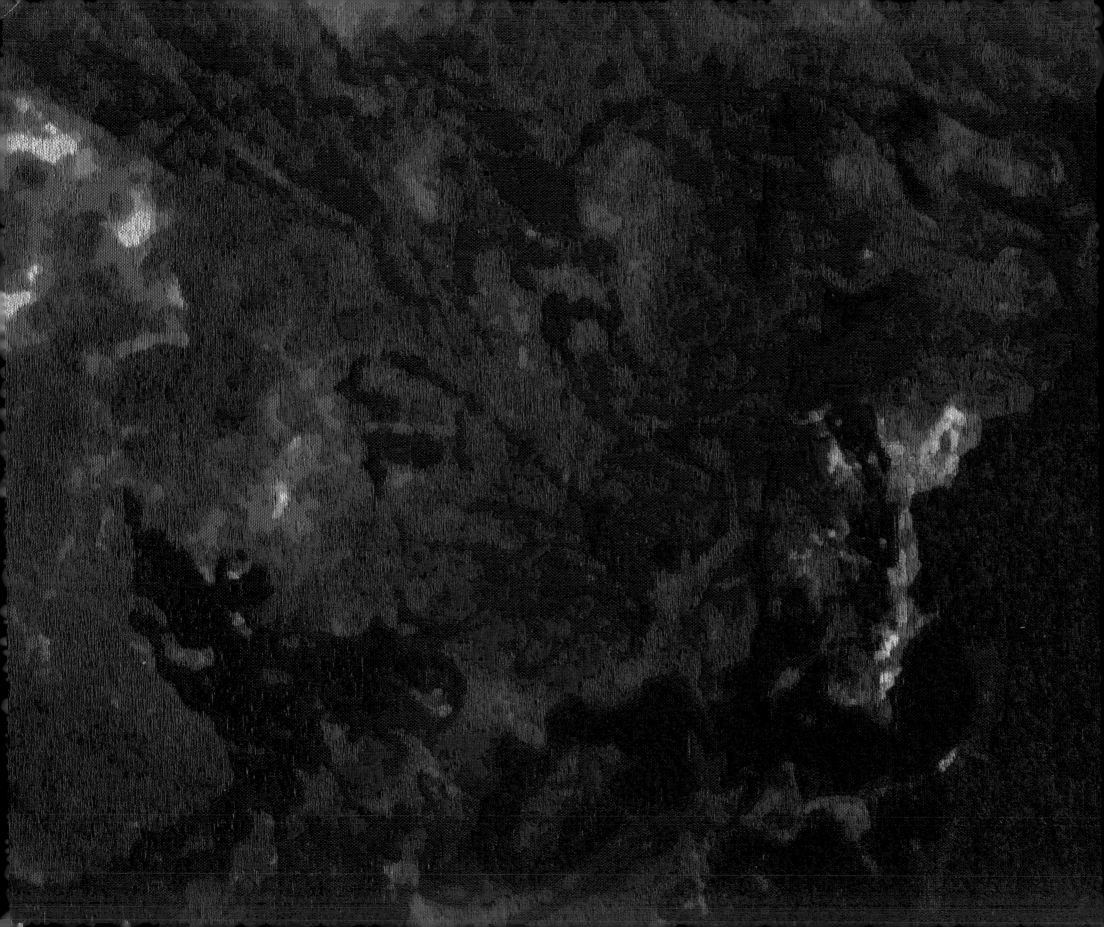

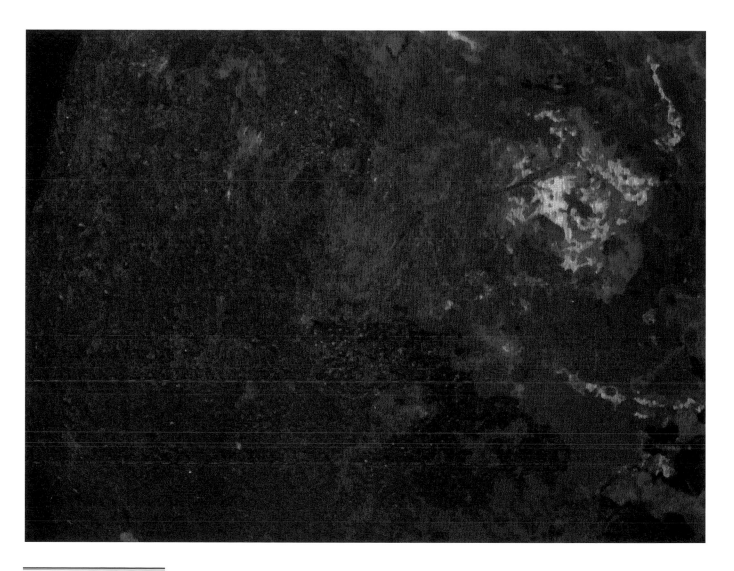

NB 10-T

2010, JACQUARD TAPESTRY
81 X 149 IN., 205.7 X 378.5 CM
REVERSE, ABOVE IN DETAIL

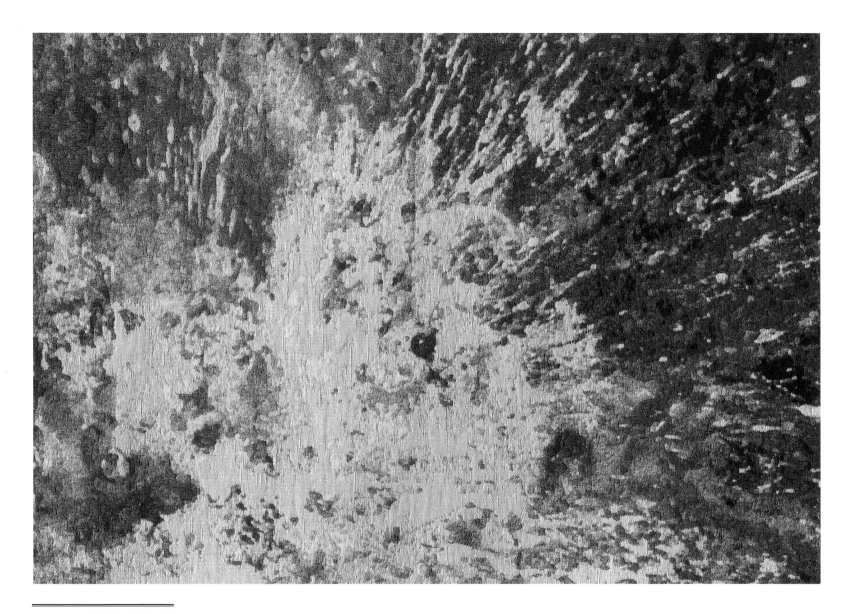

NB 01-T

2010, JACQUARD TAPESTRY
81 X 149 IN., 205.7 X 378.5 CM

OPPOSITE, ABOVE IN DETAIL

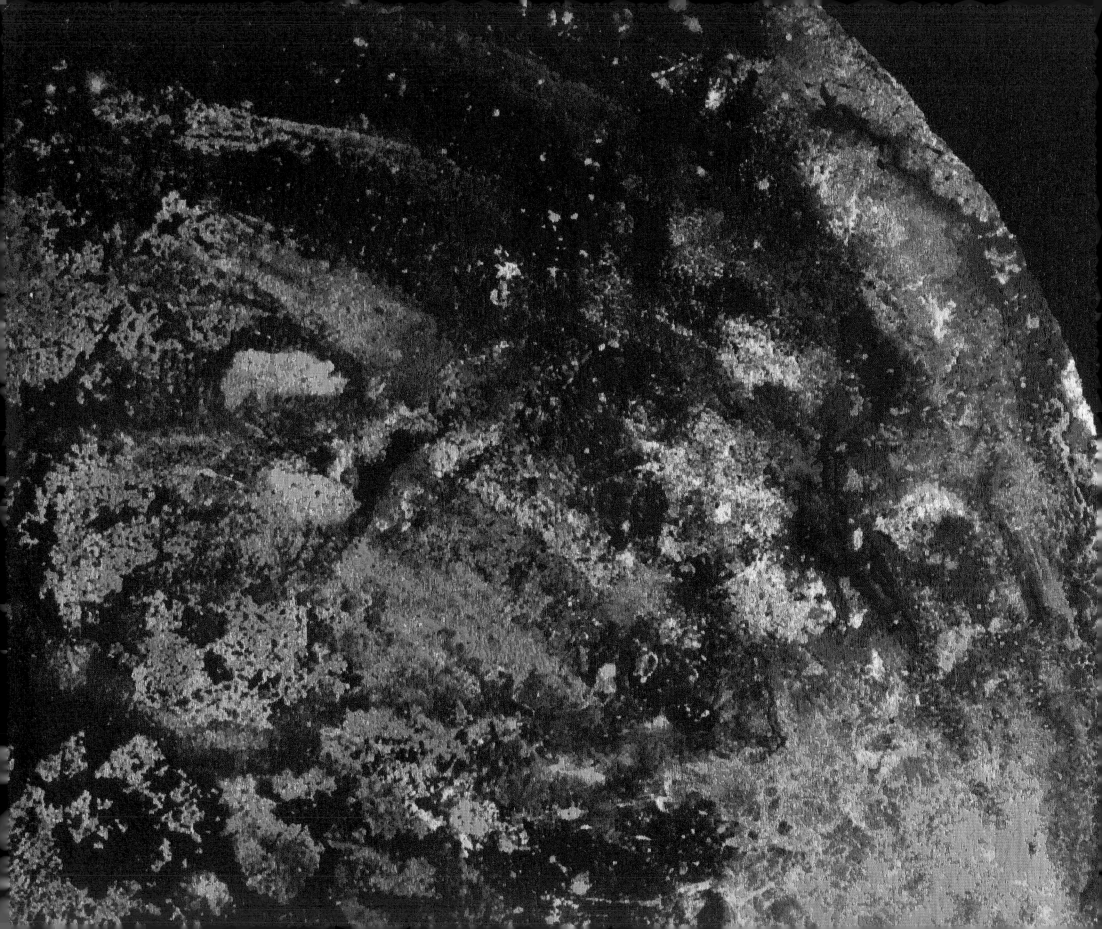

NB 06-T

2010, JACQUARD TAPESTRY
81 X 149 IN., 205.7 X 378.5 CM

REVERSE, ABOVE IN DETAIL

Monoprint 110
2010, ASPHALTUM ON PAPER, 80 X 144 IN., 203.2 X 365.7 CM

Monoprint 111

2010, ASPHALTUM ON PAPER, 80 X 144 IN., 203.2 X 365.7 CM

Monoprint 112

2010, ASPHALTUM ON PAPER, 80 X 144 IN., 203.2 X 365.7 CM

Monoprint 30, 2010, ASPHALTUM ON PAPER, 68 1/2 X 46 1/4 IN., 174 X 117.5 CM

Monoprint 31, 2010, ASPHALTUM ON PAPER, 68 1/2 X 46 1/4 IN., 174 X 117.5 CM

THE ARTIST

THIERRY W DESPONT

1948 Born in Limoges, France

1972 Diplôme d'Architecture, École nationale supérieure des beaux-arts, Paris, France

1974 MA, City Planning in Urban Design, Harvard University, Cambridge, Massachusetts

Thierry Despont is an architect, designer and artist who lives and works in New York.

As an architect, Despont has acquired an outstanding reputation as a foremost residential designer with an elite clientele in North America and Europe.
He was Associate Architect for the Centennial Restoration of the Statue of Liberty, completed the restoration of Clayton, the Frick family mansion in Pittsburgh, and designed the interiors of the J. Paul Getty Museum in Los Angeles, California.

MEDALS

1989 Chevalier de l'Ordre des Arts et Lettres, Minister of Culture, Paris, France

2000 Chevalier de l'Ordre National de la Légion d'Honneur, Paris, France

SOLO EXHIBITIONS

1992 *Illustrations for Le Bateau Ivre*, French Cultural Center, New York, New York

1993 *Illustrations for Le Bateau Ivre*, Musée Rimbaud, Charlesville, France

2002 *Thierry W Despont, Paintings and Works on Paper*, Marlborough Chelsea, New York, New York (catalogue)

2003 *Thierry W Despont, Leçons de Ténebrès*, Chapelle Saint-Louis de la Salpêtrière, Paris, France

      Thierry W Despont, Espace Bellevue, Biarritz, France

2004 *Thierry W Despont, New Paintings 2002-2003*, Marlborough Fine Art, London, England (catalogue)

      Thierry W Despont, Recent Watercolors, Marlborough Fine Art, London, England (catalogue)

      Thierry W Despont, Recent Drawings, Marlborough Gallery, New York, New York (catalogue)

2006 *Planetas*, Centro Cultural Recoleta, Buenos Aires, Argentina (catalogue)

      Masks, Marlborough Gallery, New York, New York (catalogue)

2007 *Masques*, Marlborough Monaco, Monaco (catalogue)

      Thierry W. Despont - Masks, Marlborough Fine Art, London, England (catalogue)

2008 *Thierry W. Despont: Through the Moon Door*, Marlborough Gallery, New York, New York (catalogue)

2010 *Thierry W Despont: Threading Orbs*, Marlborough Gallery, New York, New York (catalogue)

FORTHCOMING EXHIBITIONS

2010 *Thierry W Despont, Insects & Masks*, Rahmi M. Koç Museum, Istanbul, Turkey

2011 *Thierry W Despont: A Curioso Cabinet*, Location TBA, Venice, Italy

PUBLICATIONS

Despont, Thierry. *Restoring the Statue of Liberty*. New York: McGraw-Hill, 1986.

Despont, Thierry. *Houses I, II, III, V*. New York: The Office of Thierry W. Despont, Ltd. and Marquand Books, Inc, 1990, 1995, 2000, 2005.

Despont, Thierry. *Carne de Peche*. Private Publication, 2005.

Despont, Thierry. *Planets*. New York: Assouline Publishing Inc., 2005, 2008.

Despont, Thierry. *Masks*. New York: Assouline Publishing Inc., 2006, 2007.

Despont, Thierry. *Insects*. New York: Assouline, Publishing Inc., 2008.

Despont, Thierry. *Studio*. New York: Assouline Publishing Inc., 2008.

Despont, Thierry. *The Icy Moons of Saturn*. Private Publication, 2008.

Rimbaud, Arthur (illustrations by Thierry W. Despont). *Le Bateau Ivre*. New York: Thornwillow Press, 1992.

Marlborough

NEW YORK /
MARLBOROUGH GALLERY, INC.
40 West 57th Street
New York, NY 10019
Telephone 212.541.4900
Fax 212.541.4948
www.marlboroughgallery.com
mny@marlboroughgallery.com

MARLBOROUGH CHELSEA
545 West 25th Street
New York, NY 10001
Telephone 212.463.8634
Fax 212.463.9658
chelsea@marlboroughgallery.com

MARLBOROUGH GRAPHICS
40 West 57th Street
New York, NY 10019
Telephone 212.541.4900
Fax 212.541.4948
graphics@marlboroughgallery.com

AGENTS FOR:
Magdalena Abakanowicz
L.C. Armstrong
Chakaia Booker
Fernando Botero
Claudio Bravo
Grisha Bruskin
Steven Charles
Dale Chihuly
Chu Teh-Chun
Vincent Desiderio
Thierry W Despont
Richard Estes
Red Grooms
Israel Hershberg
Bill Jacklin
Kcho
Julio Larraz
Ricardo Maffei
Michele Oka Doner
Tom Otterness
Beverly Pepper
Arnaldo Pomodoro
Bruce Robbins
Will Ryman
Tomás Sánchez
Hans Silvester
Hunt Slonem
Clive Smith
Kenneth Snelson
Stephen Talasnik
Manolo Valdés
Robert Weingarten
Zao Wou-Ki
The Estate of R.B. Kitaj
The Estate of Jacques Lipchitz
The Estate of George Rickey

LONDON /
MARLBOROUGH FINE ART LTD.
6 Albemarle Street
London W1S 4BY
Telephone 44.20.7629.5161
Fax 44.20.7629.6338
www.marlboroughfineart.com
mfa@marlboroughfineart.com

MARLBOROUGH GRAPHICS
6 Albemarle Street
London W1S 4BY
Telephone 44.20.7629.5161
Fax 44.20.7495.0641
graphics@marlboroughfineart.com

AGENTS FOR:
Frank Auerbach
Matthew Carr
Stephen Conroy
Christopher Couch
John Davies
David Dawson
Daniel Enkaoua
Karl Gerstner
Francis Giacobetti
Catherine Goodman
Daniela Gullotta
Maggi Hambling
Clive Head
Paul Hodgson
John Hubbard
Thérèse Oulton
Celia Paul
Paula Rego
Vladimir Velickovic
The Estate of Avigdor Arikha
The Estate of Steven Campbell
The Estate of Chen Yifei
The Estate of Ken Kiff
The Estate of Oskar Kokoschka
The Estate of Victor Pasmore
The Estate of Sarah Raphael
The Estate of Graham Sutherland
The Estate of Euan Uglow
The Estate of Victor Willing

MONTE-CARLO /
MARLBOROUGH MONACO
4 Quai Antoine 1er
MC 98000 Monaco
Telephone 377.97.70.25.50
Fax 377.97.70.25.59
www.marlborough-monaco.com
art@marlborough-monaco.com

AGENTS FOR:
Roberto Barni
Davide Benati
The Estate of Alberto Magnelli

MADRID /
GALERÍA MARLBOROUGH, S.A.
Orfila, 5
28010 Madrid
Telephone 34.91.319.1414
Fax 34.91.308.4345
www.galeriamarlborough.com
info@galeriamarlborough.com

AGENTS FOR:
Alfonso Albacete
Juan José Aquerreta
Martín Chirino
Rafael Cidoncha
Alberto Corazón
Juan Correa
Alejandro Corujeira
Carlos Franco
Manuel Franquelo
Juan Genovés
Luis Gordillo
Abraham Lacalle
Francisco Leiro
Antonio López García
Blanca Muñoz
Juan Navarro Baldeweg
Pelayo Ortega
Daniel Quintero
David Rodríguez Caballero
Sergio Sanz
Darío Villalba
The Estate of Lucio Muñoz

BARCELONA /
MARLBOROUGH BARCELONA
València, 284, 1r 2a A
E-08007 Barcelona
Telephone 34.93.467.44.54
Fax 34.93.467.44.51

SANTIAGO DE CHILE /
GALERÍA A.M.S. MARLBOROUGH
Nueva Costanera 3723
Vitacura, Santiago, Chile
Telephone 56.2.799.3180
Fax 56.2.799.3181

//

Important Works available by:
Impressionists and Post-Impressionists;
Twentieth-Century European
Masters; German Expressionists;
Post-War American Artists

DESIGN / Maeve O'Regan
EDITORS / Dale Lanzone, Janis Gardner Cecil
PHOTOGRAPHY / Jeff Sturges

PRINTED IN NEW YORK BY PROJECT